The Ultimate Raised Bed Gardening Guide for Beginners

Maria Peretti

Hafiz Entreprises

The Ultimate Raised Bed Gardening Guide for Beginners

1

Introduction

The Ultimate Raised Bed Gardening Guide
for Beginners
Grow your own Food in less Space and Create a Beautiful & Productive Raised Bed Garden

© **Copyright 2022 by Maria Peretti- All rights reserved.**

This publication is aimed to provide accurate and reliable information on the subject and issue addressed. The book is sold with the assumption that no accounting, legally licensed, or otherwise eligible services are expected of the publisher. If advice is required, legal or professional, it should be directed to an individual trained in the profession.

A Declaration of Principles in which the Committee of the American Bar Association and the Committee of Publishers and Associations acknowledged and authorized equally that the reproduction, duplication, or transmission of any portion of published documentation in either electronic or printed format is lawful. Recording of this publication is prohibited, and any preservation of this information is not permitted unless the publisher has given written permission. All rights withheld. The information presented herein is claimed to be accurate and consistent. Any liability and terms of carelessness or otherwise, resulting from the usage or misuse of any policies, processes, or instructions found therein are the sole and absolute responsibility of the reader. Under no conditions will any legal liability or blame be expected to hold against the publisher, either explicitly or implicitly, for any reparations, damages or financial losses due to the information contained herein. The authors own all copyrights not held by

the publishing company. The information contained herein is given solely for information purposes and is standardized as such. Moreover, I am an affiliate partner of Amazon associates, If you click a product affiliate link and buy the product, then I will get a percentage of the sale or some other type of compensation from Amazon. The information in the book is provided without agreement or some guarantee. The trademarks being used are without approval, and the trademark is written without the trademark owner's permission or protection. All trademarks and labels in this book are the property of the owners, not associated with this text, and used for clarification purposes only.

FREE GOODIES FOR OUR DEAR READERS

Congratulations! You are eligible for free coloring books, self-organizing planner and many more gifts.Get Free Goodies, free books and many more surprises by connecting with us.

Just email us at: info@hafizpublications.com Or Visit us at hafizpublications.com

This book will teach you comprehensive techniques and processes on how to build a raised bed garden successfully. Raised-bed is not a new phenomenon and the advantages of growing plants have been known for decades. I know quite a few people who considered this aspect of growing plants in an upstairs bedroom but found it a lot of trouble and quite costly. However, this is far from reality, and in the long run, it is cheaper to grow something in an elevated bed than to grow in a familiar garden environment. You may have observed that I refer in particular to planting, and not directly to planting vegetables as is the usual case. The explanation for that is pretty straightforward. A raised bed garden is not only for the farming community but also encompasses the entire range of typically growing plants including, fruit growth, herbs, flowers, and, of particular, growing vegetables with which it is most widely associated. I've touched on the factors you may want to give it a little more thought – if you haven't done so already. This book is, in fact, a detailed guide for beginners on how to grow plants and vegetables that use raised bed gardening. I am quite a supporter of raised bed planting, as you might have guessed by now because it is the best way to go when it comes to development versus days consumed.

Additionally, you can easily buy raised bed gardens on Amazon and start

growing today. So, let's dive deep into it and learn the process step by step

Best Wishes Maria Peretti

Chapter 1: Understanding the Basics

1. **What is Raised Bed Gardening?**

Raised-bed gardening is a type of gardening wherein the plants in soil are embedded in two to five-foot-wide storage units (also named beds), which are typically made of plastic, concrete, or limestone and can be of any width or form. It is elevated above the underlying ground, about six inches to waist-high, and may be filled with compost.

So, what's so unique about such beds?

A raised bed is, after all, merely a plain bed that has been pulled up a little bit. However, as soon as you apply the idea to your garden, you will quickly realize their value.

A raised bed garden is not only about vegetable growers. It covers the entire spectrum of general gardening, such as growing fruit, herbs, flowers, and, of course, growing crops for which it is usually associated. There are almost as many varieties in designs, materials, and methods as there are plants that can be grown in them. Benefits of planting in raised beds instead of directly in the garden are extensive. In these beds, plants are lined up much closer together than for traditional row gardening. The spacing is such that their leaves barely reach each other when the vegetables are fully grown, providing a mild climate in which weed growth is inhibited, and humidity is maintained.

2. **The Benefits of Raised Beds**

Raised beds are an excellent solution for people who have a small garden, or don't have a garden at all. Raised beds are also perfect if you want to grow plants that need more space than the bed provides. Raised beds can be made out of many different materials, including wood and stone. They can be built in any size and shape and they offer benefits such as:

- **Eye Captivating**

  Gardens that are only planted at ground level can appear reasonably flat and without features. Raised beds improve this by increasing the planting and visually making the garden's landscape more attractive. It includes a strong design dimension, and only your imagination limits their scale, shape, or style. Beautiful beds built with cedar are an asset to your countryside.

Build perimeter gardens to spice up the entry. Moreover, grow food in the front yard and screen your eyesore. You can checkout this beautiful raised bed on Amazon as well.

- **Increased Growth**

On a practical level, elevated beds have improved drainage, and their elevation means they warm up more quickly in spring. That benefits your plant growth, mainly if you grow food crops and extend the growing season. Having a raised bed higher on one side than the other so that the sloping side faces the light, warms the bed even more effectively and encourages early growth. Building an elevated foundation reduces the amount of effort
involved in planting, making the work less back-breaking, and enabling you to enjoy the plants closer to you. That simply makes it more comfortable and enjoyable for the garden.

When using a raised bed to grow, the truth is that much of the work has already been completed, with the framework itself being constructed and filled-in. It is much easier to maintain the bed itself than the conventional gardening approach of digging a garden area and then planting it in long rows – as is the case with vegetables. Maybe I should point out here that when I say 'traditional,' this is not the case with many countries that have been using this method for centuries. In specific, mountainous areas have adopted a terraced approach to farming that is not unlike raised bed gardening. A raised bed garden is especially ideal for those with limited room to plant, but not exclusively. A small space for planting vegetables, even as low as a 7 x5-foot area, you can build a bed. It will give you a space of two feet all around the raised bed, where you can easily do the plantation.

Although the terrain for the traditional garden area is more significant, the fact is that due to the different planting techniques, more vegetables can be grown in a smaller space.

- **Easy Access**

When growing in a raised bed, you use the 'in row' method. It means the planting is much more productive in a raised bed and allows the best use of the available area. It is partly because, to care for your plants, you do not have all the excess space in walkways that you have in a typical garden! It was estimated that a traditional garden wastes up to 75 percent of the actual ground area. The raised bed system only takes up about 34%. This means that it makes full use of about 66 percent of the area available for growing it, compared to the conventional gardens. Admittedly, this isn't an 'exact science,' but I think it gives you a decent idea of how things are. However, if you have a larger area to plant in, a raised bed system is much more active. The walkway around the beds for the same planting area now serves two beds instead of one. It is merely the model of 'economy of scale' at work. Where one bed fits 9 x 6 feet in area, two beds should meet in an area not twice the size but 9 x 10 feet instead. You get a general idea, I'm sure! If you then make the best use of the available room, then it is evident that in this department, the raised bed comes up with trumps.

- **Save Time and Space**

    The beds are particularly suited to urban gardens where there is limited space. A series of high beds can help make most of the level shifts in a sloping garden, and raised beds may be used in a small garden to provide the optimum planting area. A single, distinctive raised bed (such as a keyhole garden) often makes an excellent focal point for an attractive specimen plant or even a right house. The reduced amount of weeding and labor needed to maintain them matches our "time-lack" culture of today.

- **Improves Soil**

    Where the soil is poor or unsuitable for growing certain plant types, or where you have a patio garden and therefore no soil at all, raised beds are extremely useful — nearly vital. They allow for massive soil improvement, and growing conditions can be tailored to specific plant needs, such as lime- intolerant plants. Although this can be done in a full container, the elevated beds have a distinct advantage in that there is much more space for root growth, and the soil dries out much faster and is less susceptible to temperature fluctuations.

- **Exemption from Pests**

    It's much easier to maintain pests out of a raised bed garden of all kinds than to keep them out of a traditional style garden plot. Every time the whole idea of a mesh wire barrier at the bottom of the raised bed works. The most significant pest for me is the rabbit, and the harm one rabbit can do to my vegetables overnight means they're public enemy in my house. Once again,
    the elevated bed comes up with trumps, as rabbits seldom leap above 16 inches to few feet – making it easier to keep them away from the vegetables with a simple barrier to lift the sides of the frame if appropriate to do so. It is advantageous as they cannot burrow through this

shield, because they are resistant to a fence. On another level, you already have a significant advantage: with the carrot flies, if your bed is built about 2 feet high. The reason is that the carrot fly doesn't tend to fly over 1.9 feet or so, which shows that a simple extension around your bed with a simple fly mesh to make it over two feet high means you'll avoid the worst of these pests. When it comes to things like mildness and overly sticky situations, an elevated bed can catch any little breeze that goes around. All of this helps with the internal ventilation between the plants, the lack of which is the great cause of many diseases, such as tomato plants. For flying pests like birds and moths, erecting a frame attached to the structure is a relatively straight forward solution that will enable you to add some nylon mesh over the framework and avoid pests.

It will give you easy access to your plants without all the hassle of having mesh tangled up in the plants that you may have in a traditional garden field if done with some forethought. The actual removal or treatment of pests with a raised bed is often much simpler because you are not bent over trying to find out what the problem is – it typically looks right in the face! Crop rotation is one of the key strategies for helping to prevent insect infestation. With a system of raised beds, this can be done quickly and is a sure way to help avoid contamination through the overuse of a particular growing area or plot of land.

- **Longer Growing Season**
  Another sometimes ignored benefit of this bed method is the more extended raising season with this form of gardening. Since the compost is lighter in make-up and is lifted away from the earth, this ensures it warms up quickly when the spring arrives. That means you can have a longer growth time, of course, simply so that you can plant that much sooner. A longer growing season, of course, means you will theoretically get a much higher crop. This, in turn, has a quick effect on the overall costing and can transform your growing business into a real moneymaker, helping to balance the monthly bills on food. This helps reduce and even eradicate the initial expense of setting up your garden project's entire material costs over time, from the design of the bed to the detriment of the plants and materials.

- **Perfect For Diversity**
  It is challenging to consider a raised bed growing program, without also considering the idea of 'Square Foot Gardening' – at least in the passing. This is a gardening method where each

crop is produced in an area of one square foot, and while this might sound crazy, if you haven't seen it before, it can work very well once you understand the system. The fundamental precept is to start with a four-foot framework, which you divide by string or some other simple, narrow frame into one-foot squares. This will then give you a

few squares where you can plant your different vegetables. The idea is that, as long as you rotate the planting in terms of space-time and nutrient demand, it will supply vegetables to your family during the growing season.

Anyway, it is good to see that a raised bed is very adaptable to this kind of framework. If you have more than one bed, another dimension of diversity is especially important. This allows you to focus on only one or even two crops per bed, so you can prepare the compost or fill in to meet the unique demands of that crop. If you grow carrots or parsnips, for example, then you'd make sure the fertilizer is light and loamy with a lot of sand added to

ensure the best crop. Similarly, for crops such as leeks, they needed plenty of well-rotted manure to thrive; they could be well catered in their elevated bed garden.

- **Less Weeding**

  Weeding the garden is considered as one of the less fun garden activities, although I've heard it may be therapeutic in its way. For this type of gardening, weeding the whole setup is far less of a challenge. You are not planting in a piece of ground infested with weeds but in an area of virgin territory that you specifically provided for the work in hand. I'm referring to the assumption that you didn't fill it with soil from the garden or somewhere else when you fill it in your raised bed structure (at least I hope not!). The infill of a raised bed shifts slightly depending on the crop you want to grow. It should consist of

a right compost mix, including several organic materials, such as well-rotted manure. This can be combined with some garden soil, but just about 15 percent to 75 percent compost soil. This will assist with two things; first, it will prevent the ground from compacting in the raised bed, and second, it will mean you don't import the weed seeds into the raised bed area. This all results in less weeding for you, and more time to do the more important things like picking some fresh peas for the evening meal, or plucking some canned tomatoes for that crisp summer salad! Will this mean that a raised bed garden doesn't weave at all? The simple reply is no; it's not. However, these findings significantly minimize this time-sucking chore. The soil is softer, making the weeds more comfortable to pull up. There would be fewer weeds due to the new compost you've filled in the garden.

- **Perfect For an Uneven Surface**

Raised bed gardening is nothing new, and goes as far back as the Incas and even beyond. It was not hidden from the Incas that a raised bed system can be used to make an inefficient area of the ground useful if it has too much of a slope. Yes, you might say it was more of a landscaped gardening regime, but I will respond that even the terraced garden may be similar to the raised bed, as it seeks to level a piece of ground for growing purposes. Even today, you can see this system throughout the world, particularly in mountainous regions like South America or Nepal. By using the raised bed or terraced method, whole villages can have all the vegetables they need in these mountainous regions.

So, you might not be living in Nepal! However, maybe you've got a garden plot on the side of a hill, and you've always felt that growing something there would be inappropriate? The solution is a method of raising fields, with the great team sideways to the mountain. Make one hand higher than the other to make up for the pendulum. For example, one long side maybe only 6 inches high, where the other is two feet high; if that's what it takes to level the growing surface as it should be.

In some cases, reducing the bed's width, to say, around two feet instead of three could work better. In steeper circumstances, that will be the case, as it lowers the height of the bed. When building on a hillside, one thing to remember is to make sure your frame is well secured to the ground with posts or even iron stakes. The last thing you want is to do your 'work' for gravity and take your vegetable plot down to the bottom of the hill!

- **Quick and Adjustable**

It is one of the most flexible gardening methods since it can be easily changed and adaptable to some variety of growing conditions or demands. For example, with a simple structure added with one-inch plastic tubing and some clear polythene, you can have a mini-greenhouse where you can grow fruit or vegetables, and it may be depending on where you live. This same structure can also be used to throw a nylon mesh over for defense of birds or insects; if, for example, your 'greenhouse effect' was just to last you through the early spring cold spells. Another good use of the raised-bed is to install a frame, allowing you to grow all kinds of climbing plants like pea or bean crops. Can you say you can do that with a traditional garden, too?

That's real, but it's just that much easier and simpler to build the frame and handle the crop inside an elevated bed framework. Mainly if you've constructed the bed out of lumber like most people, then it's easy to add whatever rising frame you've got to the overall elevated bed structure. If you are careful to mount this frame with screw-nails instead of just ordinary nails, this is easy to satisfy your needs without damaging the structure itself.

- **No more double digging**

At the beginning of the season, that was also one of the most challenging jobs, i.e., double digging to bring some 'looseness' back into the firm ground. This has been made secure by continuously going up and down between the rows of rising vegetables, but now with the method of raised bed planting, double digging is a thing of the past as the compost can be quickly turned over with small garden tools. You may wonder, but what about stalking the soil? This will be a problem if you are continuously growing the same crop in the situation of your bed. However, if you rotate the crops correctly, either between beds or within beds, then the compost would require little work or additives to keep it safe and so to speak 'produce the products.' One of the drawbacks of double digging is that it takes up soil at the bottom, which is still 'virgin' and brings the top growing field closer. If accurate excavation is not performed, the subsoil may be mixed with the topsoil, which is catastrophic. A network of raised beds eliminates this situation by resolving the need for double digging. The compost was already made up with plenty of organic content, allowing for soil aeration and improved nutrient distribution.

1. **Overcome Challenges in Raised Bed Gardening**

Raised beds are a beautifully effective gardening system, but they do have their specific challenges. It needs some strategic preparation and knowledge of the issues involved to make sure that the beds raised function for you. You can also use raised bed kits available on Amazon to make the process more easier.

Lifting Materials

Lifting materials to an elevated height can be a grueling job and can cause the problem or even damage if performed improperly. For example, it is much simpler to use a watering can for watering crops at a lower elevation, while it might be challenging to carry a full can to elevated bed height. There are alternatives to this, of course, such as using drainage systems or a pipe and stoppers. It may also be tougher to lift other large objects such as wheel-barrow compost loads or large plants in pots. However, low decks or scaffold panels may be used to move small quantities of compost on wheel-barrows. Conversely, only lift materials using smaller, lighter containers, such as bins. In elevated beds, tall scrambling plants such as French and runner beans or hops may be quite tricky for you to handle if you build them up with teepees and vertical structures. It means you would need to use ladders to harvest and tie in your crops. Dwarf variants of these plants, though, are just as easy to grow and will make harvesting and maintenance very easy.

Construction Cost

Manufacturing costs are much higher for raised beds than when crops are grown directly in the soil. Materials typically have to be ordered, whether using bricks, stone, or lumber. That is in addition to bolts, screws, and devices such as drills, jigsaws, and sickles to bring them together. Then, there are the planting material prices. People should have a pile of homemade fertilizer in a perfect world that could be used to cover the beds, but the fact is that so many people would have to bring material into the garden. Even then, the outlay is well worth it, as the beds can last for several years in the long term and will improve productivity with more excellent harvests for vegetable crops. Furthermore, elevated beds would minimize the need for anti-slug and snail steps, as the beds lift the production higher off the ground. It results in watering the plants more regularly than those grown in the field during the growing period depending on what sort of raised bed

you choose. This is because it offers improved drainage by raised beds. However, alternatives such as hugelkultur and keyhole gardening provide changes to the soil structure, which help preserve rather than lose moisture.

Building raised beds would decrease the amount of rising outdoor space that you have. This is because you'll need space between them to pass around. Ideally, the room should be at least wide enough to bring a wheel-barrow between the fields, leading to the loss of invaluable paths to planting areas. But, the advantage is that the raised bed can increase overall performance, and because of the extra depth in your raised bed and the improved drainage, you can plant closer together. You can reduce the amount of room that might benefit from simplifying your garden or maintenance for building some kind of layout structure.

Weed Control

Weed control at an elevated height is so much easier, but using a hoe can be tricky because of the angle, as profound perennial weeds can be dug out with a fork. Crops requiring a spade to dig up, such as artichokes and potatoes, may also be more uncomfortable to grow in the beds. It is always best to avoid strolling on the raised beds, so recognize the size and shape of the

raised bed before you construct it if you think you will need to carve over the soil. Consider carefully as to which crops are suitable for growing. Then, plants that need digging can be cultivated in compost bags, where suddenly, the packs can be torn open to harvest. Preferably you want to focus on measurements that allow you to effectively reach all areas of the bed for weeding or harvesting. You can always use a hand fork, spade, or hand hoe to dig, which can be done comfortably with precision.

Chapter 2: Types of Raised Beds

There are many different types of raised beds. One type is recycled lumber raised bed, which is a low-cost and easy way to extend the growing season. Another type is straw bale raised beds, which we have discussed in quite detail in this chapter. Another type of raised bed is called hugelkultur, which means "hill culture" in German. The soil in this type of raised bed is layered with logs, branches, and other debris to create a natural habitat for worms and other insects that work to break down organic matter into nutrients for plants. You can also checkout this multipurpose [galvanized steel raised bed garden](#) on Amazon.

There are many more, so let's read on for further details:

1. **Rooftop gardens**

   Rooftop gardens have already been famous in urban dwellers, especially those who may not have the luxury of space. A roof garden with turf and plants can cover the entire rooftop, and these are most frequently seen in commercial or public buildings. They are quite costly to build and maintain, and due to weight restrictions, not everybody can install them. Another form of roof garden consists of raised beds or containers. This is the most economical option because boxes can include all kinds of materials; even old junk can be reused. Boxes are simple to set up, require little preparation and can be quickly carried around before finding the right spot. On the other

   hand, raised beds to have a few constraints, and there are a few things to remember before you think of the vegetable patch on the deck.

As with a lawn, a rooftop is exposed to the harmful elements in the air. Nevertheless, other factors may be specific to a roof garden and not generally applicable to standard ground gardens. Once the plants are chosen for the raised beds, the location of the beds will be decided by whether the plants need sun or shade. If you don't have a flat space for roof gardening but are eager to grow your vegetables, there might be other places to do so. Trailing plants can be placed along the railings, such as grapevines, beans, and peas, or you can grow salad crops in window boxes. Every apartment or house has glass, after all. The ideal location is the kitchen window, which makes it easy to access salad leaves or herbs. Only ensure all window boxes are locked firmly. When choosing your rooftop bins, pick them in three or five Clusters. They do look better for a group of containers. Their heights are significantly more prominent, with the larger to the left. However, the sun on a rooftop is unavoidable unless shade is given by human-made protection. Heat is inevitable on a roof. Apart from the heat emitted by the sun, the heat coming out of the building is also present in the form of radiant

heat, which can be intolerable in mid-summer. Proper circulation of air under the elevated bed is essential. The wind is also a roof-gardens issue. Wind can be a monster for raised beds, just as it is for a wide range of plants, depending on the building's condition, the position of buildings nearby, and the roof elevation. Since raised beds are generally higher than containers, they may not have the roof walls protection and maybe more vulnerable to wind. If the wind is a risk, investment in the shelter may be worthwhile, either human-made or through other hardy plants which can be grown to act as windbreakers.

2. **Recycled Lumber Raised Beds**

Creating an elevated bed from recycled lumber takes a certain degree of DIY skills because you'll have to work with stuff you have saved. Planks won't always be the identical width or size, so you'll need a cautious and versatile solution. With dedication, you'll end up with a built, customizable, raised bed that will cost you absolutely nothing.

Lumber Supply

Start looking in dumpsters, and you'll find planks of wood that can be used. Always look for outdoor wood and avoid materials coming from inside houses, such as furniture or kitchen wooden cabinets, as they will rapidly rot outside. Search for old fencing bits, gravel boards, plywood sheets; even segments of sheds can be cut and used as raised bed walls.

Elevated beds can be made exclusively from posts offcuts, or upturned logs in the ground. It can be decorated with lumber to customize it and keep giving it a unique look. Often use an undercoat first, then a wood paint, or use a wood stain first. Painting your reused lumber with gentle pastel and cream colors will give a calm, muted yet elegant feel to your orchard, while bright oranges, blues, and pinks will make a significant assertion, creating the raised bed a showcase of its own. Be creative: try to cover it with colorful graffiti for an urban feel or change it to suit with a theme; i.e., black and orange colored panels on your elevated bed if you're going to have a beehive theme.

3. **Hugelkultur Bed**

This Scandinavian horticultural concept is rising in popularity as people search for new self-sustaining cultivation methods that reduce the need for plants to be watered and fed. It is based on decomposing wood. This process provides an atmosphere that acts as a sponge, retaining moisture and nutrients and releasing them when needed. It also produces moderate heat, providing warmer growing conditions, and thus early crops.

Hugelkultur means hill culture, which includes stacking up decaying logs, branches, and stones into masses and filling them with soil so that they appear like mini hills. Crops are then planted onto their sides and tops. It has been proposed that moisture and nutrient retention in hugelkultur is so strong that it could be produced in deserts, and the plants will grow solely from the goodness in the hugel bed. The beds can be as large or as small as you wish. Whole tree trunks are buried in some areas and left to disintegrate in the earth. Small mounds can be built in small urban squares with only bundles of sticks. One of the main benefits of this raised bed design is that all the content should be free because it is possible to source it locally. Practically no DIY skills are needed, too. There is no strapping or screwing of the beds together; it includes covering the logs with soil or compost using a spade.

Steepness

Many Hugel-gardeners make their beds with very steep sides, approximately 45 degrees and up to 6 feet high. The benefits are that the crops growing on the sides are at a suitable harvest height, and they have a

greater area of vegetable planting than a flatter field. It also decreases compaction in the long term, but be mindful that it produces additional shade on the north and east sides. It has been proposed that moisture and nutrient content in hugelkultur is so strong that it could be built in deserts, and the plants still thrive.

4. **Keyhole Beds**

Keyhole gardening originated in Africa but has spread its popularity all over the world. This is an innovative design based on a circular raised bed with a notch cut out of it to make it easy to reach and maintain. It has the appearance of a keyhole from an aerial view, and hence the name is Keyhole. There is a compost bin at the very center of the bed, accessible through the knotch. This slowly leaches its goodness into the surrounding soil, supplying it with moisture and nutrients. It is, in essence, a network of self- supporting raised beds. The extra creamy and deep soil ensures that plants can be planted closer together than grown in the garden.

The theory can be applied to any kind of circumstance in which the bed is raised. There's no utter need for the bed to be circular: you can play with shape. Because of the compact nature of the raised bed, their structures can be built using wires over the beds. It can be used during the summer for growing plants like runners, French beans,

or sweet peas. They can also be used during scorching weather to protect shade netting or cloths. Plastic sheeting can be pulled over in early spring or late autumn to serve as a mini polytunnel, shielding crops from frost and the severe cold. Traditionally in Africa, bed-building materials used rocks and stones to construct the outside walls, as they were in various supplies. Recycling and being planned to use whatever free stuff is available is one of the main concepts for keyhole gardening. Another advantage of rocks is that they absorb warmth during the day, making the soil warmer at night, which gives the crops faster growth rates. Other materials that can be used include corrugated metal, and bricks either laid in a herringbone pattern on their sides or cemented like a wall. Lumber may be used, but the development of a curve with it is more complicated. One recycling idea is to fill large plastic milk bottles with soil and use them to create keyhole gardens as the building blocks. Just your imagination limits you: try old glass bottles, old drainpipes, empty paint pots, or whatever you need to manage.

To fill your keyhole bed with the keyhole gardening philosophy depends heavily on having moisture-retaining soil that will provide a gradual nutrient release. It shouldn't be draining too fast or too high. Filling the bed with layers of different material types assists in providing this growing medium. Materials on the bottom layer may include wood and wood chips, cardboard; manure and compost; newspaper; wood ash; straw, and topsoil.

5. **Straw Bale Raised Beds**

For many organic gardeners, the use of straw bales in their plots is a direct answer to a question or suggestion. If your soil is so poor that you're worn out from worrying about it, straw bales may be the best option for your garden. Using straw bales in the garden as raised beds eliminates the need for bringing in a new supply of soil. There is a difference between straw and hay, and you should only utilise straw bales. Hay is just cut grass, whereas straw is the stalk. Think about it after you've planted wheat bran or other grains instead of dry grass.

Once the bales have been readied for use as a growth medium, you may begin planting. Simply put straw bales in a spot that gets plenty of sunlight and warmth, and make sure they're always moist. Straw bales are a versatile medium for gardening.

Exactly why should one resort to the method of "Straw Bale" construction? Straw bale gardening is only one method of fixing bad soil. When did you realise the soil quality was that low? To begin, contact the Cooperative Office in your area to arrange for a soil test. You may learn a lot about your soil's potential for growth and the health of the microbial colonies already there by doing a battery of tests to detect the pH level and other factors. Some farmers in the state reside in places with difficult-to-amend soil, such as thick clay or sand. Loamy soil, the optimal texture for vegetable gardening, may be created, but only after a lot of labour.

Plants in a raised bed garden are grown in a box constructed of wood or stone that has been elevated off the ground. Within its walls, plants are nurtured for human consumption. However, raised beds have the drawback of being expensive to construct and maintain. You'll need to spend money on materials for the actual construction of the foundation, and if your soil is poor to begin with, you may also need to buy bagged soil and compost to fill the garden beds. Costs have the potential to escalate rapidly. Due to the material difference, one kind of gardening is known as "straw bale gardening," or "hay bale gardening." The end result is a cost-effective method for cultivating organic vegetables in the yard.

What Stores Sell Straw Bales?

Not all of the bales are created equal. Since straw, unlike hay, doesn't contain seeds, you can use straw bales in your vegetable garden. Hay bales are often produced and sold as animal fodder. As a result, these bales often include seeds for timothy and alfalfa, both of which may germinate and grow into plants when moist. Using hay bales will cause you to cultivate more hay than

veggies. Straw, like hay, is shaped into square bales and is free of weeds. As a matter of fact, straw is a byproduct of the grain industry. Once the grain has been removed, the stalks are bundled together to form bales. Straw is 100 percent natural and, over time, decomposes into a compost that feeds your plants, so it makes an excellent garden bed. The seeds are also missing since they were removed throughout the processing steps. Many farmers use pesticides on their crops, so it's important to seek for organic straw bales.

Make sure the straw bale you purchase from a "big box" store has originated from a chemical-free organic farm. If you know a local organic farmer, you can get straw bales directly from them, but first you'll need to make sure that the bale is indeed straw and not hay. Vegetables are best planted in the spring, but a straw bale garden may be begun in the autumn. Your local cooperative extension can tell you when frost is no longer a threat in your area. The final typical frost date in your area is reflected by this frost-free date. The majority of vegetable seeds should be sown after this date. It is advisable to schedule the construction of your straw bale garden around this timeframe in order to time the planting of your vegetables.

To Find the Best Location

For your straw bale garden to thrive, you'll need a spot in the yard where it can get enough of sunlight. If you have full sun, you get at least six hours of bright sunshine every day. Some plants, like lettuce and green beans, may thrive in dappled sunshine. When deciding where to put your garden, having easy access to water is an important consideration. After being moved into place, hay bales are too heavy to move. It's going to be tough to keep up with the watering of your garden if it has to support this extra weight. If you put them in close proximity to a water supply or where you can direct a garden hose, you'll have considerably more success in eliminating them.

The Act of Planting

To kick off your straw bale garden, you'll need more than just straw bales— you'll need the right equipment. For a basic straw bale garden, you will need:
- Straw bales
- Soil or compost (If planting seeds directly in the ground)
- organic fertiliser (bone meal or blood meal in particular)
- A trowel
- Garden hose

Guide to Straw Bale Planting

Spread out a few of old magazines or cardboard boxes on the floor at the spot where you want to have your garden. Each bale's wrapping paper has to hang over to the side by a few inches.

- The paper should be covered with a bale. This would prevent the weeds from climbing to the top of the bale and invading it.
- Get the bales stacked as you want them. Make sure there's enough room

between bales to push a lawnmower or wheelbarrow through. If they get waterlogged after being set up, they will become very heavy and difficult to remove.

Conditioning using Straw Bales

Each straw bale has to be conditioned so that it may be used as a growth medium for plants in the garden. This is the most time-consuming part of the process, so don't stress! The bulk of the work is done by mother nature.

Day 1 through Day 4: Using the garden hose, water each bale well until all of the straw has been placed. Cover all with muck. The conditioning cycle can't start unless you perform this every day for three days. Bales are decaying at a steady rate. As the microorganisms begin breaking down the material, the temperature within the bale rises.

On days five, six, and seven, you should fertilise the top of the bale. Ammonium sulphate (1 cup per bale, 21-0-0) or urea (0.5 cups per bale) may be used as an alternative (46-0-0). The amounts of nitrogen, phosphorus, and potash in the fertiliser are listed in numerical format following each ingredient's name, as is normal practise in the agricultural sector. They contain high levels of nitrogen, which aid in decay and conditioning. The compost should be worked firmly into the straw after being put on each bale. You'll be talking about this cycle every day for the next three days.

On days 8 and 10, use half as much fertiliser as you used on days 1 through

1. Take care to maintain consistent watering within the straw bale.

    On day 11, you may stop watering the bale to keep it wet but should stop applying fertiliser. For the 12th day, see whether the bale has been checked. If the soil temperature is about the same as the palm of your hand, you may safely plant your crops. If the soil is hot to the touch on Day 12, give them another day without watering and check again on Day 13. You may expect the bale to be damp, but not heated.

Using Straw Bales to Grow Vegetables

After getting your bale ready, the fun part begins: planting your garden! Each hay bale is suitable for planting the following types of vegetables:
- Two or three tomatoes each hay bale.
- Cumin: 2 ounces per sack
- A bale of cucumbers may hold anything from four to six of the vegetables.
- Approximately three to four strawberries each bale.
- Plant 2-4 squash per bale.
- To three zucchinis each bundle.

It also depends on the sorts of lettuce and green beans you plant in straw bales. Before planting, make sure you check the seed packaging. Direct planting techniques are ideal for growing lettuce and beans. Pull the straw bale up to the top with your shovel. Dig a hole that's about the size of the pot your vegetable plant will need to grow. Carefully remove the plant from the container.

If the plant is stuck, you may click the jar's sides and back to free it. Do not grab the stem, since this might cause the plant to break. Gently put the straw back into place around the dirt and onto the roots as you plant the plant root- side down in the hole. I guess you could water it. To start, let me congratulate you on your successful bale garden.

Those Things That Do Not Cultivate

Straw bale gardens aren't ideal for every kind of produce. Some species struggle to coexist in this environment. Corn tends to grow too tall and noisy for a straw bale garden. Not even onions, sweet potatoes, carrots, turnips, or any other root crop does well when grown in straw bales. For the ordinary home gardener, the reward of a few tomatoes and peppers is excessive. In addition to being more tastier when produced in one's own organic, green, lush garden, these vegetables are also far more cost-effective to produce.

Straw bale gardening advice

It's important to water your straw bale garden often since the soil may dry up rapidly. The straw may last during a whole growing season. Two to four strands of rope or metal baling twine hold the bale together, giving it its distinctive form. Except on rainy days, you should water your garden every day. Plants need to be fed from time to time since they cannot create their own nutrients. If you fertilise your straw-bale garden once every two weeks while the plants are still young, you may expect a harvest every week.

1. **Ready-made Raised Beds**

    Nothing could be more comfortable than an elevated ready-made bed. Just unpack it, load it with soil, then plant or sow. There are a few different designs available, so picking a reasonable height for you to work at, will give you sufficient room to expand and blend in with your current garden style. Pre-made metal raised beds might be perfect if you love the retro look in your garden. They are usually made of Al-zinc steel panels with stainless steel fittings and safety drifting stabilized. They arrive in different sizes and shapes and are ideal for growing annual vegetables and cutting flowers. They can be made out of the kitchen door, on the patio, or even on a balcony, a beautiful feature.

Wooden raised bed Tables

When you want to increase the height of your rising crops, raised tables are useful, but don't have to fill up to the depth of a raised bed with soil. They are suitable for short-term annual vegetables such as head lettuce that are like 'cut-and-come-again' and other salad crops with shallow roots.

They are also ideal for growing strawberries, which allow their trails to hang over the edges and keep them from insects. They match small gardens, patio, and balconies in the courtyard. They are straightforward to maintain and are the ideal height to work at without leaning over and straining your back comfortably. Standard market sizes are 2 feet by 4 feet or 4 feet by 4 feet. Typically, they come 1 or 2 feet deep. Most tables often come with a thick

non-woven polypropylene cloth liner to help with fluid retention and help conserve timber durability.

Elevated troughs like raised wooden tables with high channels provide a comfortable height to grow all your tomatoes, herbs, and strawberries. They have multiple sizes, but the one advantage that troughs have over tables is the extra depth in the middle. It means depth- rooted plants, including some vegetables and sweet potatoes,

can be planted where soil depth may be as high as 2 feet. The trough's exterior edges, where it's not so deep, can be planted with shallow rooting vegetables. The base and inside of the trough will have a liner to aid with water retention and to protect the wood from degradation. Most pre- constructed troughs come with a warranty, generally for three years. They are the perfect place to squeeze into small gardens, courts, and balconies. Place it near the kitchen window, making it easy for the crops and herbs to pop out and harvest salads.

2. **Recycled Pallet Raised Beds**

Pallets are the best mate of a recycler. The wood is sturdy and robust, and cots can typically be found coming out of most warehouses or around retail stores for free. Nonetheless, always seek the owners' permission, because often pallets must be returned to the depots from which they came. Though they might look a bit rough and ready, they can be transformed into a chic or funky raised bed with a bit of sanding and painting. Tables, chairs, and picnic tables can be made from pallets to enhance the raised beds for the DIY enthusiast.

Development

- Select four pallets of the identical size to form all four sides of the bed. Getting them the exact size will make your task easier because otherwise, it will take up a lot of time trying to make things match.
- You need to reduce the height a little bit of the pallets, so they're the perfect height for your raised bed. Remember wearing gloves when doing this using a saw.
- You'll need 2 or 3 extra pallets, too. Use a crowbar to separate any of those pallets from the slats. Lay the four side pallets on the floor and screw over the holes in the slats taken from the spare pallets.
- It will keep the soil, overflowing out of the sides. Stand upright on the four sides, then screw metal corner brackets onto the inside of the pallets to hold them together to form a box.
- Line the container's interiors with a piece of landscape fabric or plastic flooring to avoid rotting of the sides. To give it an appealing capped finish, attach more spare slats along the top edges.
- Sand down the package and then paint it with the color of your choice using an external undercoat first, followed by a wood paint on the outside. Once the paint gets dry, fill the box with compost and soil under the top and plant with crops or fruit trees. Well, water the plants in it.

Maintenance

Pallet raised beds are expected to last some five to ten years. The great news is that it will cost nothing again to repair them, only a little more of your time. However, they can need repainting every few years. The soil or compost in the raised bed on the pallet may need to be weeded regularly, and it will need to top off at the end of each year as the material slowly erodes and washes away. Pallet raised beds are expected to last some five to ten years. Create this raised bed in the position it will remain as it is once constructed; it will be heavy to push.

1. **Turf Raised Beds**

    Nothing could be simpler for a purely instinctual and green up bed. You can create one out of turf-grass. It doesn't just look fantastic; it is also easy to produce. Practically no DIY competencies required. For example, if you remove turf from a section of your garden to create a path or patio, then the raised bed material is free. Turf squares are the foundations for beds and have a stable foundation. Being of naturally occurring substance, they will promote wildlife into the garden. Since the soft turf material, the sides of the raised bed often allow a comfortable bench.

Iron Turfing

To remove turf from a lawn, gardeners will use an item called a turfing iron. The head is designed like a shovel, but it's sharpened so it may be used to trim grass. Skillfully designed into the spade's long handle is a kink that keeps the tool's back edge parallel to the ground as you work, ensuring consistently sized grass squares every time. When the weather outside becomes cold, you may keep your trough out of the way in an insulated garage or beneath a deck. Protecting your channel from freezing
temperatures and drying winds is your primary worry throughout the winter months.
Plants will become dormant much like those already existent in the soil of your garden. Bring the pot back out in the spring, give the flowers a trim (if necessary), and enjoy another season of blooms. If you want to give your container garden a head start in the spring, fertilise it with [N-P-K: 10-10-10].
Excel at it Once you're done planting in the trough, a little coating of gravel as mulch will help keep the soil moist. Plants in a trough may be aesthetically enhanced by filling it with pea stones or broken bricks. The gravel would insulate the trough, making it almost self-sustaining in terms of moisture and temperature. Avoid using organic mulch at all costs, since it is very expensive and may cause crown rot in your plants. Mulch the plants and then water them in. They don't need a lot of water, so the rain that falls sometimes is typically all the water your basin will need after that. The most frequent way to kill a plant is by overwatering it. Keep in mind that caution is essential.

2. **Alpine built Trough Garden**

If you're like me and don't have a tonne of time or money to waste on annuals every year, then alpine troughs are the perfect low-maintenance, budget-friendly container garden for you. Since these designs include several alpine plants—typically dwarf varieties of well-liked shrubs and perennials—they give the impression of being sophisticated, miniaturised landscapes. Several alpine plants are quite hardy, and they thrive when planted in permeable, freezing-resistant hypertufa pots. That will save you time and money since you won't have to keep buying new plants every year.

Alpine troughs are versatile garden features that look great everywhere from a porch or patio to a pathway to the front door to the centre of a flower bed. The latter is especially effective if the trough is elevated so that it can be admired by onlookers. Troughs are a welcoming container alternative for those with limited outside area, such as city residents and apartment dwellers. Because of their compact size and low profile, most troughs may be placed in previously inaccessible areas. The process of making one of these one-of-a-kind miniature gardens is not too complicated if you remember a few basic guidelines.

Pick Your Receptacle

Have a hypertufa bucket with a hole in the bottom for drainage. In order to create hypertufa, peat moss, cement, and perlite are mixed together (recipes add sand to some). There is a wide variety of forms and sizes available for hypertufa troughs, from little pots with a diameter of 13 inches to large bowls with a circumference of 3 feet. Hypertufa's final trough is lightweight, making it easy to transport when necessary, provided its dimensions aren't prohibitive. Many gardening products contain a hypertufa pot variation. But keep in mind that if you use a container the size of a bathtub, you'll either require a forklift or perhaps some strong pals to help you transport it.

Compost and Dirt

Your alpine trough calls for soil that is one-third organic and two-thirds inorganic. Plants are doomed to decompose if the soil is saturated with decaying materials. Keep in mind that highland plants have developed to thrive on a little amount of food, favour a well-draining screening mix, and thrive in a habitat that is a carbon reproduction of the alpine zone. For the best results, combine three parts normal pot, three parts sand (bagged play sand is fine), and one part crushed shale or pebbles. Your mixture should fill up around two-thirds of the container.

Alpine Flora

Because they can thrive in several of the planet's harshest settings, alpine plants were amongst nature's most striking oddities. They need low, gritty, sharply drained soil to thrive, and are perennials found at high altitudes. They are resilient to arctic cold, desert heat, and even light rain. Water is often scarce, and melting snow, misty, or fog may be the sole source. Some plants may seem as delicate as rice paper, but they are really rather resilient because to adaptations such as their small size, which protects their buds and stems out of the worst of the weather and minimises their feeding demands. There are a few yarrows and some primroses and other alpine plants in the little corner of our perpetual garden. In addition, rock gardens work very well with Alpines.

Determine Right Plants

Troughs are essentially little perennial gardens, thus many of the same rules apply when designing a trough as when designing a landscape that is not contained inside a container. Here are some criteria to meet before selecting your plants:

- For this reason, wait until the last possible moment to choose drought- resistant plants. Since most alpine plants are hardy in zones 3–5, even the farthest zones in the United States are rather well-protected.
- Create a towering mixture in a tall container. Dwarf conifers are great for this, and I like to utilise them and then nestle slightly wider alpine plants beneath base. Choose an ultra-dwarf conifer with confidence since you might have to replace it in a few years if it grows too large for its surroundings. Also, alpine grasses might be a nice addition.
- Troughs might seem hard and harsh due of the hypertufa bowl, thus careful attention to texture is required. Tender, squishy plants are what you need to give the container a more pleasant aesthetic.
- Identify stunning plants like the ice plant and the rare grey rosette perennial orostachys. Also, don't overlook the plethora of miniature sedums and sempervivums from which to choose. Although you don't want the wider-headed forms of sempervivums to crowd out or seem out of context to the other species in the trough, it's better to stick to the miniature-headed varieties.
- Since the Alpines will be slowly rising, you should utilise trailers to fill up the empty area until the majority of the trough develops. For this reason, I like the use of creeping thymes, which may be easily divided if they become invasive.
- Plants with staggered bloom times provide continuous splashes of colour throughout the season. It's important to pay particular attention to the timing of blooms in alpine troughs since, unlike other containers,
they don't employ annuals. You may choose from a wide variety of spring, summer, and autumn flowering plants.

Choose your favourite One

Every time I pass one of those cute tiny cafes and see numerous trays of highland plants infused, I want to go home and plant them all. The people who come to my alpine-trough workshops are so enamoured with these plants that they always leave with at least two (and sometimes three) troughs. They're exactly like me, it seems, in that they need all of these plants and can't help but buy them. If I had to chose just a few plants, these would be them.

Erodium 'Flore Pleno'

It is a neat tiny ground cover that resembles a super-mini geranium (to which it is related) thanks to its little star-shaped, soft-pink double blooms with dark-pink veins. There are usually a few flowers on this 2-inch-tall beauty that blooms from late spring into summer.

Sempervivella

Its popular name is "sempervivum," after the genus Sempervivum, since it resembles a full-grown sempervivum. Foliage creates rosettes in a surprising variety of asymmetrical clusters. Orchids ranging from white to light yellow, typically with red streaks, bloom on 8-inch tall stalks in the spring. This is a sturdy option if you really want to add some luscious texture.

Ice Plant, Named "Starburst"

'Starburst' is a 4-inch-tall ice crop with glossy green leaves and vivid, hot pink blooms with white centres throughout the summer. It thrives in full light and makes low-fat, tasty leaf cushions.

Get the plants positioned and the roots prepared

When I remove a plant from its bowl, I take out about half of the root ball and gently release the rest of the roots. The plant's growth will be momentarily slowed as a result of this. Each plant may be tucked into the trough at the ideal soil level, with space for the fresh roots to develop underneath, since most basins are quite shallow. In their enthusiasm to share the adorable plants with others, many individuals make the common error of trying to fit too many into a narrow container. You want saplings to be put so that they are at minimum a few inches apart. You may also fill up any empty spots with a few of colourful rocks.

When the weather outside becomes chilly, just tuck your drill away beneath the deck or in an empty apartment. The toughest part of roosting is preventing your trough from being blown away by the dry, cold air. The plants will hibernate just like their surface-level counterparts in your garden. In the early spring, remove the container, prune the plants (if required), and let them to drain and rebloom. You may give the container a little boost in the spring by fertilising it (N-P-K: 10-10-10).

Closed-Top Dressing

A little coating of gravel should be used as mulch when you have completed cultivating the trough. The trough's plants may be highlighted by placing them on a bed of tiny pea stone or shattered brick. The gravel helps to retain in humidity, rendering the channel nearly independent. To prevent rot at the plant's top, organic mulch of any kind should be avoided.

After you have completed mulching, give the plants a gentle soaking. The alpines can survive on very little water, so the rain that falls sometimes is all that your trough will require after that. The most frequent way to kill a plant is to overwater it. Remember, the key is to maintain a state of calm contentment.

3. **Woven Raised Beds**

This form of elevated bed is perfect for a cottage garden and has a charming feature. One of the ancient methods of construction is the use of supple stems to build structures. Many medieval edifices were created using a wattle and daub technique, centered on branch weaving wattle to construct it. It was resurrected during the early twentieth-century interior decorating trend, and this traditional, rustic technique has recently resurged in the garden once again.

The advantage of using versatile willow branches is that it's easy to build curvy sides as straight edges on the raised bed. So, in terms of shape, you can be as imaginative as you want. One of the oldest types is the use of supple branches to build structures.

Setting a Woven Bed in your Garden

- One clear path where the bed will be raised, and mark the texture of the foundation on the ground is by using sand or string.
- Use a sledgehammer to tap substantial wooden stakes into the edges of the ground. Additionally, put sturdy hazel stakes along the sides every 20 inches or so. Willow may be used, but chestnut and oak are all you need.
- Browning them briefly over a flame will harden the wood, which will make it last indefinitely in the soil.
- Take the lengths of the young willow stems and weave them in between the posts, placing each branch next to one position and then beyond the next one. When the next row is started, place the branch on the opposing side of the post to where the one underneath it ended.
- As the willow is working around the framework of the raised bed, it is necessary to keep pressing it down to keep it as close as possible. The bed can be at the height you wish.
- It is good lining the inside with an agricultural cloth liner or black plastic sheeting before

covering the bed with soil and compost, due to the rapid perishing aspect of the woven-bed structures. That will increase the life of the willow branches by a few more years.
- If you want to make an original raised bed wattle and daub, you need to get a little dirty. The woven part is called the wattle; it is the daub, the muddy material that makes it watertight. Straw, soil, cow manure, and freshwater are the four essential ingredients.
- On a wooden board, mix the first three materials in equal proportions and add the water — traditionally, this would have been incorporated by the feet of the craftsman, or by animals for large structures. Using your spade to incorporate the daub thoroughly should be enough here to make it a thick, yet flexible material.
- The daub is picked by hand and, starting at the base, "splattered" or tossed onto the woven frame. Then the palm is used to smooth it out, forcing it through any crack. The daub should be about one and a half centimeters. Go and take a shower, at last!

Maintenance

The woven material has to last two or three years and then needs to be replaced. It will last longer than a few years. Substitute the content by simply extracting the branches and repeating the process after a few months. Branches newer and more flexible. The older branches can be shredded or chipped, and then added to the soil's surface to serve as mulch, helping to preserve moisture and suppress weed.

1. **Bulk bags Garden**

Large woven bags from builders make excellent, easily raised beds, which can be put as a feature anywhere in the yard. These are also called bulk bags,
the large white bags used by builders to drop material to household homes and building sites containing materials like topsoil, gravel, and compost. They typically have a capacity of 1 ton, but other sizes do exist. They may look a little rough and ready, but to see free-cycled products modified to be used in the garden is lovely. If you like, you can create a wooden board around one, then clothe it with thinner wooden pieces to make it look a little smarter.

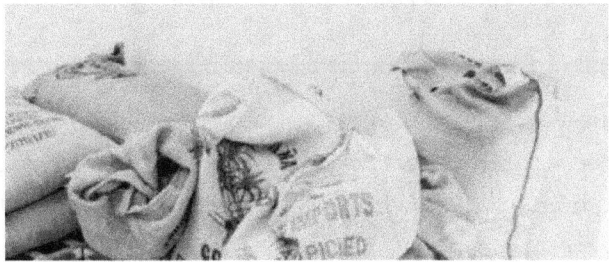

Why do they use bulk bags?
Commonly, the bags are safe. Ask about building sites or facilities as they are typically more than ready to get out of them. They are made of great content and are expected to last a few years. When the sacks are loaded, they are charged on a great working height. When filled with soil or

manure, they have good depth, meaning deep-rooted crops such as carrots, parsnips, and leeks can be produced. They are versatile as they are mobile. After harvest, in a different position, empty the soil until relocating it. The substance is porous so that extra moisture will drain off naturally — you won't have to worry about the drainpipe at the lower part.

Fill in the Bags

If you don't have space for a bulk bag, then you can use plastic containers. Start growing potatoes in a 20-gallon compost tank. The sides of the compost bags can provide some security from the dreaded potato blight: rolling the bags up significantly higher than the stems decreases the likelihood of

landing immediately on the plant species of fungal spores. Potatoes are to be planted in the middle of spring.

- Cut small drainage holes inside the compost bag, if there are not already some.
- Roll down the sides of the compost bag to make it around 8 inches tall.
- Put about 4 inches of the soil underneath the container.
- Place two potatoes on the manure, facing upwards with their "heads."
- Cover a further 4 inches of soil over.
- As the potato shoots expand, the bag should be rolled up to a height of 13-18 inches and top off with compost.
- Water the potatoes daily, but do not overdo it; otherwise, the tuber will rot.
- The bag will be torn open after the potato plants have flowered, and the potatoes harvested.

Maintenance

Bulk bags will last three years or so until they need replacement. They will need frequent weeding each year. Every year, these packets must be overlaid with fresh manure or soil. In warm weather, bulk bags may be susceptible to drying out, so always check to see if plants require watering. You may exploit the deep soil too. Plants from the cucurbit family are going to do well as long as there is plenty of rich compost. Start growing the squashes or pumpkins. A few should be enough up in the center. It can then hang down the length, disguising the bulk bag's woven fabric. Conversely, eight tomato plants may be planted around the corners and trained on a stakes system, making it easy to harvest.

Place your Bag

Consider deeply about where you are going to place your bulk bag before filling it with compost because it's tough to move a 1-ton suitcase once you've put it on. To lower the fertilizer needed to fill the bag and make it lighter, fill it half with the polystyrene bits left over from the packaging.

Before topping off with compost, cover this with plastic sheeting so that the compost does not fall between the polystyrene pieces. The bag will be in the highest possible sunshine, ensuring you can cultivate a wider variety of plants.

Chapter 3: Designing Your Raised Bed

1. **Finding the right Area**

Finding the right area is among the significant decisions you'll make when you commence your garden to a raised bed. You have to start giving your plants with the right conditions to flourish, so bear in mind these essential location factors. You can also check right kind of raised beds on Amazon, as per your requirements.

If the room is small, don't worry. Position your beds up on your patio if there is adequate daylight. Raised-bed gardening generates comparatively high yields, meaning that due to various factors, you get more production from less space. Pretty early in the year, the soil gets warmer, allowing the plants to grow quicker. Plants are brought closer together than in rows, so you have more plants to produce. Generally, you leave 2 to 3 feet between rows in conventional gardening. You use this area for planting with raised beds. You can make your soil mix instead of attempting to boost the same soil, which leads to higher yields.

2. **Shaping the bed**

Quickly, what's the first thing that comes into your mind when you hear the word "Raised beds" I mean, except a mattress slung over the open ceiling rafters? The typical picture is a, and for a useful purpose, wooden box in the shape of a square. The most frequent type of raised bed is a four-square-foot structure. For most backyards, it is also a practical option and is easy to work with. But not every room lends itself to a series of square foot beds. And besides, you may want to be a little more imaginative than that, particularly if you're going to garden in your suburban front yard without neighbors blowing your whistle on you. I present a few types of raised beds in this chapter to help you think – beyond the square wooden box.

High Beds

Any garden bed that is more than two-foot-high is what I call super-high. It is often designed for looks that way, particularly as part of landscaping in the front yard. During a super-high raised bed that I built in front of my home, I was sick of pruning the three rows of hedges that had been planted in that area by previous owners, and so had taken them out. After replacing the beds in the backyard, we finalized with a bunch of leftover landscape edging bricks. I was looking for more space to grow lettuce, and since that specific area gets sufficient sun in the spring and fall, when we can produce lettuce in that climate, I decided that I wanted to create a raised bed there. We designed and constructed a mattress to match the existing boundary of landscaping, carefully arranging the bricks in it. Since I only wanted to grow greens there and had enough blocks, I also filled the center of the bed with cubes, leaving only enough space at the top to put in six inches of potting mix. Since the roots of lettuce grow shallow, this was deep enough.

When we eventually realized to dig out all the grass on that side of the front lawn and bring in a mix of perennial herbs and landscaping plants, the super-high bed rendered a heavy accent in the back, from the sidewalk view. We stacked the bricks freehand, but many people built these beds with mortar between the brick rows. That is not, of course, the only way to create super-high raised beds. They may have wooden walls too. There are also square boxes of wood on the legs to make them table height. Such beds are designed primarily for work-friendliness, most commonly used by old or disabled people who cannot bend or sit down from a six to a twelve-inch high bed. The issue with these is that you can only make them so deep – typically six inches – and you are very limited as to what you can expand. The two main advantages of super-high raised beds are their appealing looks and ease of working in them. The big downside is the cost. It would add to the expense to have to put more in between the bed. Neither would it be inexpensive to create these beds out of wood, because you would have to pick rot-resistant boards.

Keyhole beds

Keyhole beds have become a perfect option for people who want to expand their front yard in various vegetation. But, they need to be careful about how it looks. They're also ideal for people with a postcard-sized yard because you can fit a few more plants in them since they're round than you can do in a rectangular bed with the same space. Keyhole beds can be constructed as low or as high as you wish or need; their shape is unique.

Here's how you build that bed:

- First, put a stake in the ground center of the area that you intend to turn into a garden bed. Add to the stake a five or six-foot-long line, based on whether you want a ten or twelve-foot diameter bed.
- At the end of the string, move slowly around the stake, marking each foot or so with a stone or stick to signify the perimeter of the room.
- Anywhere you want the bed's entrance, generate a stone path that stretches eighteen to twenty-four inches wide to the bed's center.
- You will be able to reach all but probably the outermost plants from this direction. Get rid of the grass and fill the bed with organic material after selecting and building a boundary around both the outside of the bed and along its edge.
- It's enough to say that a keyhole bed's beauty is that the shortest plants are moving along the road, with the larger plants behind them, and everything is within easy reach.

Herb Spirals

Herb spirals are a unique type of raised bed that is enormously successful among the permaculture community because it saves space and water, creating multiple micro-climates in one limited depth. The spirals allow you to grow a lot of herbs in a relatively small area and a wide variety of herbs with different light and water needs.

How can you make one for you?

Build a mound of soil that is three feet high and five feet in diameter. Position rocks about a baseball's size into a basketball – the largest ones at the bottom

- in a hexagonal pattern, starting from the bottom and winding upward. Between every tier, there should be around a foot of soil. Plant herbs that appreciate the sun and are tolerant of droughts, such as oregano, garlic, and onion, are on the southern side near the top. Peregrine and chives prefer less sunshine and colder temperatures, so plant them on the north. Water Loving herbs should be at the bottom, like mint, because you can start watering at the top of the spiral and let it flow down.

While this name implies that this gardening technique is for herbs, I say, why not try it out with conventional vegetable crops? Also have at top one broccoli, one Swiss chard, three kale or one okra, because they are relatively drought-tolerant. Further down, a few carrots and a little bell pepper plant planted with bush beans. At the very edge, grow lettuce, as it is one of the dirtiest cultivated vegetable crops. If you want to plant in a spiral of herbs, it makes for a stunning piece of landscaping in the front garden or a quiet – and aromatic – focal point for a backyard vegetable garden. The premise of this chapter is that you can build raised beds from any shape and at any height you like. Concluding with two pieces of advice: if you want – or need

- to create more than four feet of rectangular beds, keep them three feet long, and make sure that you can reach them from both sides.

Whatever the shape of the bed you create, ensure that you have at least two feet of walking space between the beds. Now that you have some creative ideas about the kinds of raised beds that you might create, what are some excellent building materials for it?

1. **Choosing Right kind of Materials**

   A raised bed can be built around any material, as long as it is sufficient to maintain the soil. Evite products that may contaminate the soil and thereby impact plant and, possibly, human health. The creosote and tar present in the ties can affect the ground, and contaminants such as asbestos are harmful
   carcinogenic substances.

Budget, material availability, and personal taste are the key factors that should guide you in making your choice.

Wood

Wood is relatively inexpensive, ready to use for home improvement stores, and it takes only simple DIY skills to create a raised bed using it. Hardwood is more durable than softwood, but pressure-treated softwood would have a longer lifespan. Gravel boards are useful because they are light and reliable, and if more compost or soil is added, additional boards can be added each year to provide more space. Railway connections offer an enticing, chunky, rustic feel to an elevated bed, and give a rather robust

foundation. They are sufficiently wide to get a seating area as well, which can be a valuable tool to rest on after a workshop of digging or weeding the bed. But be careful to use old recycled railroad ties, as they can drain creosote and tar into the grounds and pollute the soil. You can purchase new railroad ties through log merchants, either hard- and softwood and they'll cut them to your size.

Furthermore, wooden pallets, logs, or old scaffold panels are useful resources that can be used for building raised beds. Pallets also find themselves outside garden centers, warehouses, and factories. Often check with business owners before you help yourself. The surplus logs would also be available to tree surgeons and garden companies. Look at scaffold board recycling websites or purchase from home improvement centers. The biggest downside of wood is that it will inevitably rot and require replacing. Bricks and metal will last a great deal. In the style of wood, you might find reconstituted plastic, which will produce a similar appearance to wood and have much higher stability.

Bricks

Bricks are the right material to use for an uplifting room. A certain degree of bricklaying ability is needed, and the bed will need footings to keep the walls against sinking, and capping on top to prevent additional egression. However, it will be worth it as they are hard-wearing, and your brick raised bed will last long. They can be shaped into anything you need/like with a bit of creativity. There are various types of blocks to choose from in a variety of colors, but it's typically better to select ones in line with the environment. For example, if your home is made of red concrete brick, select these for your raised bed. If you have an old fashioned cottage made of mellow yellow bricks, then it might be worth tracking the same color of new, reclaimed bricks. The downside to using blocks is that they can be costly when you choose to purchase them. Start looking at local recycling and trading websites for the community, because you can also find second-hand bricks for sale.

Breezeblocks are thicker than bricks and are simpler to build. If left un- rendered, they may look slightly unrefined, but if that doesn't concern you, they're a great inexpensive alternative to bricks. Rocks, stones, and flints can reuse materials from your yards to build up the bedsides. Artisans typically build drystone or flint walls using a lime-based mortar to keep them together.

Metal

A metal raised bed in a classical garden might look very chic and stylish. The reused material can be located and used regularly. Seek to visit nearby scrapyards and see what content they possess. From corrugated metal sheeting to old metal waste bins, almost everything can be used. A metalworker or engineering firm can cut metal sheets to any shape or size. Be conscious that the metal will get heated in summer, and the bed will need additional watering towards the sides. The foundation would be colder throughout winter than those made of wood or stone, which may be a problem if it's in a cold place.

Natural materials

Even elevated beds can be made from sod piles, from soil formed into concrete slabs, or from wattle and daub. Straw bales also became a common choice for growing plants in the kitchen garden. Knitted material such as cinderblocks or woven hazel or willow may be used to build a cottage garden's feeling, which will last for a few years before replacement. Bear in mind that although natural materials can look very appealing, life expectancy is often decreased.

Willow Panels

Raised beds can be built from willow panels to make typical kitchen gardens and to showcase an attractive feature. At each end of the group, the panels should be fastened to vertically wooden stakes, either with string or wire or

nailed into place. Online or from most garden centers, you can purchase the plates.

The material is natural and unregulated and will last in the garden for a couple of years. Willow panels should not be too thick because they will not be sturdy enough to withstand a large amount of soil: it is suitable for around 10 inches high and 4 feet long. If you're just growing annuals, you might take them down in winter, store them in the barn, and take them out the next year. That should help prolong their lifespan. They can be used in their own right as raised beds, or they could hide an uglier substance such as plastic by using it around the outside as "dressing." If you use them as a bed, install a liner inside to help preserve your life.

Recycled materials

There are tons of recycled materials that can be used to build a raised bed: from a rubber tire to an old sandpit, everything. Old roof tiles or bricks on their edges may be forced into the dirt, making a low bed. Also, a scrap car's chassis and frame can be used to grow plants in.

2. **Construction of Brick Raised Bed**

Brick raised beds are more complex to build than wooden ones, requiring much more practical knowledge such as bricklaying, but still very easy to learn. If installed, they will last a lifetime and provide a reliable, stable bed that looks great in most locations, be it a garden front or back yard.

- Use string to mark out the bed's perimeter. Install concrete footings. That will prevent the sinking of the surface. Dig out a 20-inch deep trench and two bricks long.
- Cover the bottom with a concrete base consisting of one part cement, two-and-a-half parts sand, and three-and-a-half parts gravel to 6 inches wide.

- Enable to dry and then mix the cement, using three parts of sand to one part of cement. Water should be applied to make it an easy-to-use consistency, which is not too messy but adequately flexible to spread over the brick-work. The application of a plasticizer helps to preserve the cement.
- Start laying brick courses, two bricks wide. Bed each block up onto a 1-inch cement sheet. Start the new layer with half a block to balance the blocks with the courses underneath, which will make it more durable. Using strings and a level to ensure a standard for every class.
- Three layers at first take you to ground level. Continue over the ground until you reach the desired height.
- Chamfered coping brick pairs should be cemented to protect against dampness all around the top edge to make it appear more appealing. Line the walls within with permeable membrane.
- Add topsoil and compost.

If you have more than one upstairs room, you'll have to think carefully about the paths that go through and between them. Paths form the backbone and framework of any garden design and are essential for achieving the main elements of the garden. They need to be fully operative and practical, but ideally, they should look good and fit in with your elevated bed style. For example, a formal brick raised bed with a rustic wood chip path around it can look incongruous.

Bricks or Paving slabs

The most stable paths should have a sturdy foundation to move your wheelbarrow along. They can be simply laid in the soil for a rustic look, digging them down to the brick or patio slab depth, so they're flush with the earth. You can bed them on sand if you like, and then brush them in a dry mixture of sand and cement to keep them cleaner. Water it gently to let the mix set. They can be in different sizes and prices to match the budgets of most people. If you're not thinking about style, then check out dumpsters, because you'll see people throwing out old bricks and paving slabs. You should check with the homeowner or developer, of course, before rummaging through their dumpster.

3. **Plan and Construct your Raised Bed**

Making a Rooftop Garden

Before preparing to build the roof-top raised beds, it is necessary to remember that permission should be obtained if a landlord owns the roof. Beds are massive structures to set up, which require a lot of work. If the landlord or other tenants object, it is difficult to remove them. You also have to observe the building code. Because of the fire risks, roof gardens may not be permitted on the rooftops. The raising of all the materials onto the roof can also require permission. It is not an easy job to raise tons of soil to a four- story building and requires proper preparation and coordination.

The Planning Phase

Once permission has been granted or is unnecessary, weight is the first thing to consider before constructing the beds. Considering that the beds raised will not be built from concrete blocks, soil, particularly wet soil, may get very heavy. A rough estimate of about 1.200 Kg per cubic meter for dry land, or

2.100 pounds per cubic yard. The roof-top can be put under a lot of pressure, depending on the desired size or amount of raised beds.

The soil's density and weight differ, and the easiest way to quantify the possible load is to test a sample of the clay used, both dry and wet. Then measure according to the bed's inside dimensions. Apart from the soil, it is essential to consider the weight of the raised bed itself, the weight of the plants which will grow in it, and any other structures which already exist on the roof. If a protective membrane is mounted on the roof-top, it does not take too much to drag on harsh materials. An additional layer may be added to protect the membrane, and this would also add to the roof weight.

A nursery or landscape designer should have the knowledge if the roof can withstand the weight, possibly after an inspection. Alternatively, the architect of the building should be able to provide detailed guidance. The architect will also direct you where appropriate to provide additional structural support to the roof-top. It is essential to assess structural damage accurately as it is a real possibility, and it can be quite exorbitant to repair, mainly if the roof is not owned by you.

You should also consider during the planning phase about the type of plants that will be cultivated in the beds raised. For vegetables or other edible plants, such as herbs, care must be taken to ensure that the material from which the foundations are produced does not spill into the soil, potentially adding unnecessary chemicals and contaminants that can be ingested by the plants. This may be bad for the plants but bad for human consumption as well. It should be water-resistant if the beds are made of wood so that it does not deteriorate with repeated watering.

Implementation

The elevated beds are substantially large containers. They can consist of wooden boxes, concrete boxes, half-cut barrels, or even old bathtubs. High beds are elevated off the ground, and they should have ample clearing to permit adequate drainage and air circulation. If the foundations are not lifted from the earth, they can cause significant water damage to the property's roof as water sits down and flows through the stone.

- Nowadays, there are many houses with small extensions, usually at the rear. If you don't intend to walk on it, you just want to put some pots or containers to admire from your couch; then, it can't be any clearer.
- Select attractive looking boxes that suit the design of your own house. You can use aluminum for modern home and the traditional terracotta.
- Position crocks or wire mesh over drainage troughs. In the bottom, to avoid blockage of drainage holes upon the soil.
- Add compost to general purpose and plant some with colorful plants or good ones. Water the plants well, then keep watered periodically
- Summer holidays

The Gardening Project:

Once the beds raised are ready, soil and plants filled and protected from the elements. There is something that can become evident very quickly is a water supply or the lack of it! It's best to have a water link or some kind of water storage on the roof, depending on the size of the raised beds. Going up and downstairs and lifts, filling up buckets of water can get very tiring. When there is no water link, a barrel of rain may be placed on the roof. Space permitting, building a storage room for all the gardening equipment will also be a smart idea. Things such as watering cans, fertilizer, soil, and gardening can be stored in a small closet on the roof and available where appropriate. Better than remembering you've forgotten your compost, and to get it, you have to go down three stories!

Maintenance

Vegetables should be selected routinely in a roof-top garden to keep them generating more, and for the perpetuation of the display, ornamental plants will require deadheading. During summer, keep plants well-drained. They could be more vulnerable to drying out from the excessive wind due to its higher condition, so check periodically to make sure the soil hasn't dried out. Holding the beds free of weeds is necessary.

Create a Hugelkultur bed

- Remove the turf from the region where the large beds are to be placed. Save the bits of sod for afterward. Cover the existing soil to a depth of approximately 12 inches.
- Save the land for later. If the topsoil and subsoil differ clearly, then take them away too. Wood and stack logs in the trap, with the strongest at the bottom. Use rotted, as well as un-rotted timber. The more forest you bring into your house, the more nutrients and water it offers, and the longer it lasts.
- Construct the wood level up to approximately 3-4 feet above ground level, depending on the height at which you wish to elevate your bed. Wrap layers of up-turned turf and the subsoil over the logs. Move some of the soil between the timber gaps to get the rotting cycle underway.
- Fix the sides and tops with compost or topsoil. Sculpt and rake the ground to form it as a mound.
- Now, you're able to plant. Most people plant annual vegetable crops, but it is possible to use enormous beds for perennials, shrubs, and trees.
- If required, the sides of the beds can be finished off with lumber lengths. This provides the bed some definition and may prevent nearby weeds from creeping onto the huge bed.

Maintenance

The maintenance of this bed is very little because they are such a self- sufficient one. After a while, the foundation will begin to sag as the timber starts to rot, so more soil will need to be applied, and the slopes re- contoured. Young plants, especially in the first year or so, will require extensive watering to create them as rotting timber benefits may not be immediately present. Check any weeds periodically, and be prepared to eradicate perennial plants before they have a chance to establish themselves. Besides that, very little is to it. Hugel beds should not, as a rule of thumb, be dug over like a typical vegetable bed, as they depend on the natural soil structure in the rotting timber. Some applications of soil may be required for eliminating weeds and planting. Still, it should be kept to a minimum, with the introduction of compost and green and brown content to the bed surface, allowing the worms and rain to carry it down to the root system.

Construct a Keyhole garden

- Clear a space for the garden to construct keyhole. You will need space for the actual Keyhole Garden, but you will need room for access around it.
- Drop any remaining weeds. For a keyhole garden, the ideal diameter is 10 feet, as this enables you to enter all segments of the bed without standing on it. Keyhole beds may, however, be any size that fits your garden area. They are usually round, but if you wish you could play with the form.

- Put a bamboo cane in the center where the bed is raised, tie a string to it and add another bamboo cane to the other end of the series at a distance of 5 meters. Use this guide to scratch out the contour of the raised bed.
- Mark out a circle knot, around one-eighth of the total area. This notch lets you reach the middle compost bin.
- Use a fork to dig into the soil to break down any compaction. Next, begin building the exterior wall. Almost any good quality material can be used, but it is rocks that are the typical material. The average wall height is around 3 feet, but this can be varied according to individual needs.
- Now build the compost bin for the bed center. This is produced traditionally by weaving flexible sticks or canes together. Willow or bamboo will do well. However, a tube of chicken wire or wire mesh with a width of about 2 feet and about 4 feet high is much easier to make.
- Secure it in place using pushed mesh bamboo canes. Line the insides of the outside borders of the raised bed with cardboard or straw, then apply layers of recycled polymer and wet it down as you go. The last few inches are lined with weed-free topsoil. To attract water and moisture towards the outer edges, the soil will slope down from near the top of the basket to the outside wall.
- Apply different layers of brown and green waste to the compost bin, such as cardboard and kitchen scraps. These provide humidity and
nutrients for the plants. Don't leave space for adding new content that fills it. Your garden is now ready to plant. Water the seedlings freshly planted, or any seeds that are sown.
- Seek to stop watering the plants daily; however, infrequent watering pushes the roots down into the bed core to make them self-supporting.

Maintenance

Keyhole raised beds are self- supporting and easy to maintain. Crops will need less watering than conventional elevated beds, although, during hot weather, you should keep an eye out for wilting plants. Water the compost bin occasionally; the moisture, in turn, would leach out into the plants. Plants might require additional irrigation, however. This would be particularly the case outside the beds as they are farthest from the compost heap and are thus more
likely to dry out and suffer due to lack of nutrients. Thanks to the increased fertility and nutrient content of the soil and convenient composting method. Dig them out the moment you find them. You can simply add annual weeds back into the compost bin, but perennial plants should be disposed of elsewhere. Keep the compost bin regularly topped off with green waste in the kitchen, grass clippings, newspaper, etc. The entire thing comes to a halt if the container starts being "fed." In Africa, roofs are also given to the compost bins (usually thatched from straw) to keep the compost moist, to stop them from drying out, and to speed up the decomposition process.

Make a bed raised from recycled wood.

- Use strings to mark up the bed shape. The bed may be whatever the size you want, but no more than 4 to 7 feet. You can stretch a few feet without even walking on the ground to reach the center of the bed.
- Following the form, catch trenches, which are half the depth of the posts used. Since these will only be assisted by soil, this extra depth is necessary without bracing anything.
- Using a rubber mallet, bang them into the ground to ensure they are upright. Cut the four corners from the reprocessed lumber with a saw (remember to wear gloves) for your raised bed. Drag them outside.
- Continue adding the thirds and screw them onto the posts as you go. Finally, to make them look neat, cut the positions flush to the edge of the raised bed.
- Conversely, you can end up leaving the posts uncut so that nets and frost cloth can be draped over as a frame. Do not start making your recycled lumber raised bed taller than 20 inches anyway because the bracing and frameworks will be needed to hold the posts together. Sometimes, that style is called a palisade.

Maintenance

The lumber is a sustainable bed that will last around 5-10 years, based on the type of wood used. Softwood is not going to last as long as hardwood. Gradually the soil or compost breaks down and leaches out, and at the end of the year, it will typically need to top off with new content. If the bed contains annual plants, they may need to dig out in late autumn or early summer before replanting them to top off with soil.

Make a Raised bed of turf

Turf sod pieces can be purchased from a sod farm or garden center, but recycling slices of grass from your garden area would be much better.

- To hack down on a half-moon (a garden tool used to slash through turf), create rectangular forms of about 12 inches across the turf about 20 cm. A turfing iron or spade is then used to cut horizontally from the
roots to a depth roughly 1.5 inches to leave you with turf slices. The building blocks of your elevated bed will be these.
- Mark, where the foundation will be erected using string or just sand. Don't forget that if you build an upstairs bedroom on an existing grass, then strip the turf below and use it to make up the walls.
- Start laying the pieces of sod along the proposed outline of the lifted bed, with the grass facing downwards.
- Build the layers up to their desired height. The structure is expected to be more reliable if bits of sod, like brickwork, are spaced. Using wood pegs or stakes and smash them in the middle of the turf wall.
- To help hold the sod in place every meter. First, put a 1-inch layer of topsoil for the final base. The dumpling should be placed on the top floor, but this time is facing the grass upstream. Firm the turf down so that it lies below in the topsoil.
- When this is over, water the sod to hold its top green-gray. If the bed raised was installed during the summer. Most days during dry periods would need to be watered for the first few weeks until it's fixed.
- You can use wire pegs if you wish, and you have spare turf pin additional strips of grass to the sides of the pad. To a final flourish, if you don't want to use the top as turf seats, you may want to sow a wildflower mixture into the sod for a more color splash and for more animals to draw.
- The raised bed of turf is now ready for use. This can be achieved with compost, topsoil, and planting.

Maintenance

Relatively the Turf fields are maintenance-free. They will last for years, although they will slowly sink as the soil decomposes and erodes gradually. However, you can maintain the height of the raised bed by merely applying fresh turf to the top layer. If you wish to keep the grass trimmed, use a string trimmer every few weeks during the growing season is best. Occasionally you may want to eradicate some annual weeds from the turf walls, such as

dandelions and daisies, but you may be happy to keep them as an extra splash of color.

1. **Planting, Watering, and Composting**

The planning is already in! If your plants grow in their raised bed or fail to produce, it is mostly down to how well you organize the soil when planting. When growing in normal conditions, cultivating a raised bed is very comparable to planting a flower border or vegetable patch. However, plants are sometimes planted closer together in a raised bed, especially in deep foundations, as roots are assumed to go further down.

The soil or manure should be adequately prepared before planting starts. All plants have different growing requirements — such as distance between plants, sunlight and humidity, and type of soil — and some are more specific than others. Usually, there is data on the seed packet or crop label that you can test if you're unsure about it. If plants have already been expanded in the soil, dig them over and eliminate any perennial weeds. To prevent compacting the land, it is generally safer not to step on raised beds. Still, depending on the bed's height and width, it might be necessary

to lay boards or scaffold panels across the bed to reach the soil, provided the raised bed is strong enough to bear the weight. When crops are to be planted, then applying well-rotted manure or garden compost supports the soil. Work this down, rake the soil level, and let it settle for a couple of days.

Don't crowd your rooms. Because the soil level will drop slightly, if beds are filled past the edge of the bed, groundwater will then spill out. Have soil level about 1-3 inches below the bed top. Mulch or compost will still top the rates out later in the year. You'll probably like to add mulch or compost every year to improve the soil, so it's a good idea to leave a gap. If plants climbing structures include runner beans, scrambling roses or clematis are needed, then it is best to have these first to prevent later trampling over the plants. Structures for climbing can include teepees, trellises, or archways. It is essential to give the plants an excellent watering first, before trying to plant anything at all in the raised bed. Lay the plants in trays, moisture the soil until it is saturated, and afterward leave them in the containers for about an hour to soak up any more water if needed.

Organize a planting hole in the bed make sure to remove each plant from its pot to shorten the length, as the root ball is subjected to daylight and thereby reduce its chances of drying out. Once the sowing hole has been dug, it should ease the plant.

From its bowl, if the plant is root-bound, the origins should be taunted out to help stop it from proceeding to spiral around once it has been planted, as this will strangle the plant at long last. This is more essential for trees and shrubs because they have a higher life expectancy than herbaceous plants. More Influenced, the rest of the trees and shrubs will not be planted in-depth in the earth than in the bowl. It is quite critical to verify that the plant species are at the proper distance from each other for planting. If you're unsure, then check the label of the plant. The point is after the plants have evolved to their own. The correct height for minimum exposure to soil. This is because the bare ground will allow weeds to germinate, and the torrential rain will cause leaching of any nutrients.

Watering

Plant matter in raised beds would need more irrigation than plants explicitly grown in the field because of the extra drainage offered by the raised beds. The extra warmth of an elevated bed and the exposure to wind would also cause the soil to dry out more quickly. Seedlings must be kept well-watered in summer, or else they will start wilting speedily and possibly even die. Water shortages are the primary reason plants die in the garden. There are some methods to reduce the amount of water the plants would require. Seek to avoid leaving bare soil in the elevated bed as the moisture evaporates quickly. Alternatively, cover with a mulch like garden manure over it. The digging into the ground with organic matter would also help to preserve moisture. Choose plants that can withstand dry conditions. Most ornamental plants can withstand dry conditions, like grasses, bamboos, and plants of typical North American prairie form.

Irrigation

Take into account utilizing irrigation in the yard but avoid sprinklers, as they throw lots of water into the air and often don't hit the target. Instead, use soaker hoses that lie in between the plants on the surface of the raised bed and softly trickle out water across the root system. They can be installed on timers so that they will only produce water for a short time. It's easy to make a home-made soaker hose by perforating an old tube with small holes using a fork. Evite mid- day watering of plants. This can result in water evaporation before it has had an opportunity to percolate down into the roots. It can also cause scorching of the leaves if the midday sun catches wet leaves. Watering is most active at night (though prolonged dampness may attract slugs during the evening) or in the morning. If possible, stop watering with a hose as water may be lost due to splashing excessively. Too often, it doesn't hit the root system directly; instead, it splashes over the leaves, flowers, and surrounding areas. If possible, using a watering to target the area around the roots, specifically. Put new mounds of soil around a plant in a ring to form some sort of bowl that can then be filled with water. This keeps the water around the roots in place, ensuring it doesn't drain away from the plant.

Taking up Rainwater

Staying on top of watering during the summer is crucial. With environmental issues and the expensive effects of water meters to some people, collecting as much rain as feasible for use in the garden is preferable. It seems a pity to witness all that rainwater wash away from the drainage systems, but then have to reimburse the spigot for it. It is possible to install rain barrels to retrieve the rain, funneled, and guttering that comes off the roofs. Guttering can be easily fixed to any garden buildings and infrastructures such as a greenhouse or shed.

Use a tape measure to calculate how much plastic ducting would be needed to catch all rainwater. First, use a pencil to mark the hut where the barrel of rain should go. That is where the guttering outlet would need to be placed. The rain barrel can be put outside the shelter, usually to the side — make sure the doors are still open.

A string can be stretched around the shed as a guideline to decide where the guttering will begin and where it will end (by the water outlet), maintaining a very slight tilt so that rainwater drains away. Drill pilot holes at 4-foot intervals in the side of the shed and screw duct brackets to protect the gutter.

Both ends of the guttering should have slotted end pieces on to prevent rainwater from flowing from the terms. The guttering is then clipped into the frame. Place a barrel of rain below the gutter. It should be brought up from the ground, for example with bricks, so that watering can fit

Tap to the bottom of the barrel underneath. Use a tape measure to determine the distance from the gutter outlet to the top of the rain barrel and cut the pipe down accordingly.

The downpipe is attached to the gutter outlet at the top and the rain barrel cloth at the bottom. Using a bracket, add the downpipe to the shelter. Finally, once a barrel of rain has filled in the winter, it is a good idea to have a second barrel, and even a third barrel, which will capture excess water from the first barrel. To do so, it is possible to add an outlet pipe to the downpipe to store surplus water. The water will flow naturally into the surrounding rain.

Composting

Every attractive garden requires a decent composting structure, and it does not have to be either complex or high-tech. Not only is it independent, to transport it in large pouches, but you also wouldn't have to keep driving to the garden center, and your home-made fertilizer will be better and more natural than any item you can buy. Composting is a beautiful way of utilizing kitchen and garden waste, and the consequent healthy, nutrient- rich manure can be assigned to the soil in your raised beds. There are various types of composting systems available, including keyhole and hugelkultur, which concentrate on plant material's biodegradation process to feed the raised bed. Compost bins could either be introduced as part of the raised bed or installed in a separate garden area.

How many heaps?

If space permits, three compost heaps are ideal in a garden (although two are workable): one to bring rubbish, one to be rendered to rot, and a third to be used on the raised beds, that is already spoiled. Keep the manure covered to prevent rinsing and leeching off of the material. Check the heap, however, to make sure it doesn't dry out. If it does, then add the stack with water.

Ideally, biomass heaps should be turned biweekly with a fork to allow air to enter the material, which will accelerate the decomposition process. But it's not necessary as you might shut it down once a year, it's going to take longer to decompose the content. Place an empty organic waste bay next to the heap where possible, so that it can be started turning into the vacant bay and left. Having compost of suitable quality requires the right balance between the two main ingredients, carbon, and nitrogen. Optimally, two parts of coal to a piece of nitrogen would be the balance. Carbon is supplemented with material such as the dry leaves, wood chips, and bark as a newspaper. Nitrogen is derived from green material such as grass clippings or yard waste, such as herbaceous plant material. If the manure is stinky and slimy,

then it possibly contains too much nitrogen, and more carbon content needs to be added and mixed in. When the compost is too dry and not decaying, there is too much pollution and need to add more green waste. Water may also be introduced from the rain barrel. The optimal mix for most plants to grow in a raised bed is 50 percent topsoil and 50 percent garden compost, but there may be specific requirements for more advanced plants such as alpine or acid soil-loving plants. The fertilizer is ready to rot into a brownish, crumbly substance and has a rich, earthy aroma of woodland. It does not smell nasty or feels too damp and slimy.

2. **Planting Projects**

Raised dahlia bed

Originating from Mexico, dahlias favor to be situated in full sunshine, but a considerable portion of shade will be tolerated. They utterly despise being in the wet soil; however, as their fibrous root systems begin to rot, good drainage is vital to growing them successfully. High beds provide an optimal situation for thick, clay soil gardens, as the altitude allows excess water to flow away and allows you to add improved drainage characteristics to compost or soil. Dahlias are prone to slugs and snails, so their growth off the ground will limit the damage. Rabbits have a remarkable ability to dig up the edible tubers — putting them out of control should help to prevent that.

Construction

There are many unique dahlia types; the hard part will be selecting which ones to bring into your room.

- Build your bed upright. Any bed structure will do but ensure that if the garden has poor soil, it is raised off the floor by at least one foot to increase drainage.
- Fill the raised bed with high-quality manure or topsoil and apply a 50:50 blend of horticultural grit. This should strengthen drainage, and prevent rotting of the tuberous root.
- Pick a range of different variants. There are heaps to choose from but to maximize the effect, get a mix. Don't think too hard about color clashes; this adds to the right, cheerful effect with dahlias.
- Plant dahlia tubers at a location of about 20 inches across each tuber with different varieties, when the probability of frost is over. They should be 4-6 inches deep beneath the surface of the soil.

- Water the tubers well and water them well before new growth starts. From then on, water them only every few days, if the weather has stayed dry.

Maintenance

When the tubers begin to develop their tips, a puffier plant that will yield more flowers should be pinched out to promote. This is generally when they reach around 15 inches in height. Use a combination of pruners and cut back the leaves to a fresh pair. For maximum impact, retain only 5 or 6 shots that grow directly off the main stem. This will ensure that the petals get to a decent height and don't get too crowded. Remove any shoots above the foundation. As the dahlias start to develop, they will need to stake to avoid flopping over the large flower heads. Through summer, feed dahlias with a healthy liquid fertilizer once every two weeks. If you are living in USDA hardiness zones of seven or lower. Therefore the tubers should be pulled out of the ground once the foliage begins blacking in the fall. Take them into a shed and hold them inside out for a week or two to dry, to permit any excess.

Drain out moisture. Place them in containers and protect them for the winter with sand or manure, and keep them in a frost-free position like a garden shed or greenhouse. When the risk of frost has over, plant them outside again in late spring. When you garden in USDA zones eight or higher, it isn't appropriate to dig up the dahlias; just cut the foliage back once it's scorched. The application of an extra 3 inches of mulch to support the soil above the tuber would help to provide added support.

Wildlife Pond

Building a pond is among the best wildlife events you can do and is a perfect way to draw more tourists to your area. "Garden ponds are important for the wildlife," says Freshwater Habitats Trust. Around 479,000 ponds are believed to be in the British countryside, but many are endangered by pollution, erosion, and development. Nonetheless, an estimated 2.3 million

backyard ponds have been built by British gardeners, which together provide substantial habitat. It would take few days to create a wildlife pond, but it can produce results quite quickly. "Create a pond, fill it with groundwater, and in a few hours, wildlife will begin to appear in the form of flying insects," says Kathryn. "Plant it with wild species placed closer to home to make sure you have the safest native surroundings for local species, and you'll get an existing wildlife pond within the next year or two. And creating a pond in your yard would also attract more birds, animals, and invertebrates.

You're going to need:
- Pitch
- Seagull Liner
- Plants in pond
- Turf, or stone
- A line of sand or gravel

Steps to follow:
- Choose a shaded garden area away from elongated trees. Mark a contour, then dig no further than 30 cm. Include slanting edges for planting and smooth shelves.
- Use a level of spirit that rests on a plank to verify that both sides of the pond are at scale. That means all of the membranes will be immersed and shielded from the sun until the pool is completed.
- Remove sharp stones, and use old carpets, curtains, or sand to create a safe underlay. Slice the liner to fit, and there is plenty of space for depth. The rubber liners are flexible and robust.
- Cover grass or stones to the top of the coating. Attach a layer of clean sand or gravel where plants can gain traction and fill it from a water- butt using rainwater.
- Intermediate and floating would leave plants better and good when forced into the water by small-rooted plants. Submerged plants require reasonable quality of the water.
- Offering a mixture of long grass, log piles, and rocks can allow frogs to live year-round and provide stop-off points for frog let dispersal. Timber slabs or strips should protect newts and frogs.
- Many animals and plants live at the edges of the shallow water, thereby having a 25–30 cm deep pond with slightly sloping sides that will provide the best environment for amphibians and invertebrates.
- Talk of it like a fish in a bath. Such animals want dense vegetation, which provides a place to hide and attract other creatures, which are a vital source of food.
- Enable grasses and plants to trail across the surface of the pond. This will give water beetles excellent habitat. Garden centers store native plants for cooling. Look for the 'Be Plant Wise' tag, which shows responsibility for their sourcing.
- Get species that are already growing in the area, so seek freshwater sources within 30 km of your home and be sure you ask approval from the land-owner, if necessary. Naturally, you can let seedlings populate, but this process may take several years to complete.

Sunken Beds

For other fields, such as those in arid, dusty climates like the desert, sunken beds only fill in the necessary crop-based evolutionary connection. Although raised beds facilitate better drainage, sunken beds are built to maximize water accumulation and hold the moisture until the plants absorb it. Although raised beds bring the plants up to the sun during the day, sunken beds offer a little protection from the swelter. While raised beds thaw out more quickly in frigid climates, sunken beds keep stuff more relaxed in the heat. Sunken beds can be troublesome in arid climates prone to flood events, as they are slightly geared to flooding, taking full advantage of sparse rainfall instead of draining water away. In this case, creating drainage outlets might be wise, so that the beds do not occasionally overfill with water, drowning the plants.

How to make this bed?

A further positive thing about sunken beds over raised beds is that they don't demand that you buy or collect materials to build the boundaries. You just have to dig in. The bad news would be that the soil is dry and hard to dig in most environments right for sunken beds, mostly with layers of caliche (hardened calcium carbonate deposits) that look like concrete. Besides, the layers of hardened earth are part of the issue, drinking up rain resources quickly when it falls. In other words, hard work or not, you may need to call in a pickax. If the soil in the region is low, as is the case in most arid climates, then it would possibly take about 2 feet to dig out, eventually saving some topsoil to bring back into the garden bed. Once the hole is in place, it should be refilled up to about five or six inches below the ground surface with a mix of quality, moisture-retaining soil and organic compost. Adding a proper layer (three or four inches) of mulch to avoid the water from dissolving is essential at the top of this. That's a sunken bed, just ready to go.

If sunken beds seem to be the right fit for you, then here are a few other thoughts and methods that may be helpful. If the soil is severe, then cover the area with mulch before attempting to dig it, and then wait for rain or

water it from the house using graywater. The humidity softens the room and makes the excavation much easier. Note how water flows on the property and suggest building channeling structures to areas where gardens (or swales) are using the infertile excavated soil. It will make that much more of the amount of water that is caught.

Use it (the excavated dirt) to build short walls around the garden bed that will give young plants shade and protection from the wind—the efficient design of the sunken garden, fully utilizing the space to create an oasis. Consider having a sunken keyhole design for shade, stability, and biodiversity, or building a native plant forest (not in need of drunkenness) around the garden. For those who have the practice and experience to do so, sunken beds can be recycling pits for the first time, swallowing up organic household waste for a few months, so that good soil is developed on-site rather than trucked (or bagged in). Get organic matter, details, and materials free to help initiate the fertility process.

3. **Dealing with Pests and diseases**

Many growers face bugs throughout periodically in their vegetable garden, and they are not typically that big of a deal. Nevertheless, pest numbers often rise to an utterly unacceptable rate, and the little buggers do more than mere aesthetic harm. When gardeners are more conscious of the possible risks of exposure to artificial insecticides, many of us tend to avoid the sprays entirely and then turn to other strategies for pest control. In the first instance, the most productive method for managing garden pests is by far stopping them from nibbling on your plants. The extraordinary thing is that it's beneficial to avoid pests in your orchard then you think, if you use the five very successful methods I outline below.

I was a toxic pesticide "junkie" when I qualified from college with a degree in gardening. I used a wide variety of synthetic pesticides to combat pest insects in my yard and the fields of a few hundred clients. I decided to stop splattering synthetic materials and go organic when a friend and colleague horticulture started suffering the unhealthy effects of exposure pesticide poisoning. Indeed, I still used natural pest control products for many years
after that, including horticultural oil and pesticide soap, but then I started using those items too. For the past eleven years, I have not splashed anything in my orchard to regulate pests, not even organic pesticides. I have a lovely garden, and I appreciate the role that parasites play in my countryside (they are food for the good bugs!), and I use steps to protect them in check before their harm gets out of control.

Attempting to prevent pests in your garden:
Foster advantageous insects. While pollinating insects are fantastic to have in the garden, the beetles that I'm talking about here are the ones that take a real bite out of insect pests. Ladybugs, lacewings, little pirate bugs, parasitic insects, damsel insects, and other benefits keep the overall number of pests down by consuming the bad guys for brunch or using them to shelter and raise their babies.

To attract these useful bugs to the garden, you need to provide them with protein-rich pest bugs and carbohydrate-rich nectar to be eaten as food. But, not just any flower serves as a source of nectar for insect pests. We need a particular form of floral architecture to spring nectar from. Here's a description of some of the best indigenous natural plants. The more effective insect-munching you have around, the less likely it is to get out of hand for pest numbers. The whole point is to create the right balance. Here's an excellent guide if you'd like to learn more about attracting beneficial bugs to your garden.

Beneficial insects are useful for avoiding outbreaks of pests

Attracting beneficial insects to your garden, like the ladybug, is a perfect way to prevent plant pests from catching on. Pick your plants wisely. Some plants and their varieties are more susceptible to pest problems than others. Pest control is often as easy as selecting pest-resistant crops in your yard. For example, if squash bugs continuously attack your winter squash plants, the

two most resilient varieties are 'Butternut' and 'Royal Acorn.' Or, if Colorado potato beetles still try to defoliate your tuber crop, plant 'King Harry' potato (a Cornell University bred variety) with very hairy leaves that the beetles will not consume. Hunt out varieties of other vegetables resistant to pests and diseases, too.

Prevent squash bugs by selecting hardy varieties

The collection of types goes a long way to avoiding squash bugs. Similarly, young plants can be protected with hovering row cover until they reach bloom. External obstacles are used. Placing a physical barrier between the plant and the insect is one of the most effective strategies to avoid pests in your garden. Cover plants prone to pest with floating line cover, a compact, spun-bound fabric that lies on top of the crops or wire hoops. Please ensure the protection contains plenty of slack and pin the surfaces to the ground to prevent sly bugs from creeping under the edges. I use a row cover to keep cultivated cabbageworm caterpillars off my cabbage, broccoli, and kale. I also include my young bean plants to discourage beetles from Mexico, my young cabbage plants to hold the cucumber beetles in the bay, and my new squash plants to avoid squash beetles and borers. Only remember to remove the row shield when the seeds germinate into the bloom to allow pollinators to reach it.

To Prevent Pests from Attacking Plants, Use a Floating Cover.

Protect garden pests by shielding floating row covered plants. Intended to prevent pests can also be the primary factor in determining the uniqueness of your vegetable patch in your garden. Parasites will have a more difficult time finding their host plants by cross-planting different leafy vegetables with each other-and with flowering herbs and annuals. Instead of planting a suitable species in a row or block, mix all together to hold even small monocultures outside the garden. Although there is still much analysis of correctly how planting works, this technique appears to "confuse" the pest insect. Some pests might have to land on the plant a certain amount of time

to locate and verify that a specific plant is widely respected. Once crops are interpolated, the pest can fall on a different species of plants each time, making it quite complex for the bug to home in at their dinner. Dill is an excellent crop to draw beneficial bugs. Plants with flower heads and fragrant foliage are great plants for intercropping and enticing beneficial insects, such as this dill.

Grow medicinal plants. It may seem a unique case, but this is the essential method of preventing pests in your garden, in the view of this horticulture. Like you and I, plants have an immune system (although one that is unique from our own), and when plants are stable and unstressed, they are, of course, less attractive to pests. Furthermore, healthy plants have a whole range of great tricks to deter pests by using their chemical protection mechanism. Given your best prevention steps sooner or later, there is likely to be an outbreak of pest or illness in the garden. If you are taking time to determine what kinds of control measures you find appropriate for your garden, you will be better prepared to deal with any problems that might arise. Are you going to take a hands-off approach and let nature run its course? Are you going to limit controls to physical methods like barriers, traps, and handpicking? Consider using insect sprays or fungicide sprays? Will you only utilize organically acceptable pesticide controls? Do you consider using pesticides of a synthetic chemical nature? Who will have the responsibility for the application of pesticides? No one approach is right or wrong; it's whatever works best in your setting.

Frequently check your plants for initial signs of insect and disease. Solving a small issue in the bud is much easier than controlling a severe one. By merely knocking the insects off plants with a steady stream of water from a hose, you may be able to stop a small aphid infestation. If you wait until your plants swarm with aphids, it will take more drastic measures. On the other hand, when not needed, don't pull out the big guns. Be sure that the number of pests and the harm they do justify the degree of control before resorting

to insecticide sprays. It isn't necessarily beneficial to exterminate all pests. If you enlist the aid of beneficial insects, they need to feed some of the pests around or start moving on to greener pastures. It is necessary to compromise where there are enough pests to benefit, but not so many that cause unnecessary harm to your crops. Be sure to correctly identify which pest or disease you are observing to know what control measures, if any, are appropriate. Do some study to see the life cycle of any pathogen or infectious disease and the most productive stages in cycle treatments? Keep in mind that most problems are caused by bad weather or rising circumstances, not insects or species with diseases. Solving these problems means changing the ecological conditions that led to them, and not using pesticides where possible.

For example, find physical controls. More giant insects such as tomato hornworms and Japanese beetles can be handled relatively easily by handpicking (if you are squeamish, just wear gloves!). Selectively picking insects is best when the weather conditions make them sluggish in the early morning or evening. Throw away them by putting them into a container of soapy water (the soap breaks the tension on the top of the sea so that they cannot escape). Collecting and disposing of infected leaves at the outset can monitor the spread of some diseases. If a situation is difficult and you want to use a pesticide is needed, bear in mind these points for safe and successful use. The healthier the plants are, the more they can fend off all of the pests themselves. Feed your plants by feeding a balanced organic matter diet on your soil and make sure they are planted in conditions where they can grow (plants in the light, shade plants in the shade, etc.). One of the most straightforward steps to avoid pests in your garden is growing nicely, safe plants.

4. **Maintenance throughout the Year**

There have been a few critical jobs to do during the year to ensure that your raised beds appear in tip-top shape. Little too often, this is the easiest way to

remain on site of garden maintenance. Interestingly, even in winter, when most plants are inactive, and most of the plant beds are dry, there are always plenty of garden chores to do.

Plants on Stack

Throughout early spring, many ornamental plants may need staking to keep them from flopping over the boundaries of the raised beds and onto the pathways. The trick to making it look standard with staking is to get it in place before it's too late. It is better to let the plants grow through the staking system instead of attempting to keep the plant upright once it has begun to flop over. For the latter case, it can look fake, unnatural, and trussed up tightly. The staking products shall include:

- For example, Brush can be used to create a stunning rustic structure between the beds built from birch or willows.
- Chain stakes can be bought online or at a garden center. Generally, they are plastic or metal and attach to go across the plants.
- Single-stakes are also used to support young trees and bushes with fruit.
- Netting may be tightly placed between posts, so that plants may crawl through them.
- Small sticks or twigs are suitable for scrambling through peas and some types of beans.
- Willow teepees can be used for sweet peas or French and runner beans preparation.

Deadheading

When flowers have begun to fade, they must be withdrawn to allow the plant to redirect their energy into new flowers being created. Roses and sweet peas respond exceptionally well to this and, if regularly deadheaded, will continue to produce impressive floral displays throughout months. This is the easiest way to do garden maintenance throughout the year.

Conclusion

For all of the purposes discussed in this and other books, I am a massive fan of raised bed gardening. It's difficult to find a drawback to this type of gardening, unless you may want to incorporate, first the work and expenditure of setting up a raised bed. Having said that, though, it does cost several dollars to set up. Everything is safe in this life, and anything you commit to doing is typically costly in time, resources, or just plain cognitive thought! But the bottom line is that gardening, whether in an elevated bed situation or just an everyday backyard situation, has a lot to commend. Gardening is pleasant for soul and body, from growing flowers to beautifying your life and the lives of others, to growing crops to support your family and even the rest of the neighborhood! Several projects have now been set up to promote, in particular, raised bed planting to put together entire communities. Growing up and doing your hands' work has a real, lasting value in every culture, and is an amazing way to socialize with your neighbors. Even children seem to have a particular inclination to work in the garden, mainly if you educate them early before the teen spots start! This can be an effective method to build up genuine respect for your children's environment and the way things are, not as they are on television or the store shelves.

References:

- Earth easy Guides & Articles. N.d. *Raised Garden Beds.* [online] Available at: <https://learn.eartheasy.com/guides/raised-garden- beds/>.
- Nolan, T., n.d. *6 Things To Think About Before Preparing A Raised Bed Garden.*[online]SavvyGardening.Availableat: <https://savvygardening.com/preparing-a-raised-bed-garden/>.
- The Spruce. n.d. *15 Beautiful And Practical Raised Bed Garden Designs.* [online] Available at: <https://www.thespruce.com/raised-bed- garden-ideas-4172154>.
- Gardener's Supply. N.d. *Guide To Raised Garden Beds: Plans, Timing,*

Tending|Gardener'sSupply.[online]Availableat:
<https://www.gardeners.com/how-to/raised-bed- basics/8565.html>.

- GardenDesign.com. n.d. *Raised Bed Garden Design: How to Layout & Build-GardenDesign.*[online]Availableat:

<https://www.gardendesign.com/vegetables/raised-beds.html>.

Hey Friends!

How has been your experience after reading the book?

Hope that this book improves your life, health and wellbeing. Your precious feedback would be of great value for us and help us improve. Thanks and Stay Connected with us for FREE Goodies at:

info@hafizpublications.com

Visit us at : hafizpublications.com

www.ingramcontent.com/pod-product-compliance
Lightning Source LLC
Chambersburg PA
CBHW081627100526
44590CB00021B/3642